Discovery Kids

CUTEST CATS OF ALL TIME

by Mari Bolte

PEBBLE
a capstone imprint

Published by Pebble, an imprint of Capstone
1710 Roe Crest Drive, North Mankato, Minnesota 56003
capstonepub.com

Library of Congress Cataloging-in-Publication Data
Names: Bolte, Mari author
Title: Cutest cats of all time / by Mari Bolte.
Description: North Mankato, Minnesota : Pebble Emerge, an imprint of Capstone, 2026. | Series: Cutest of all time | Includes index. | Audience: Ages 5-8 | Audience: Grades 2-3 | Summary: "Each cat breed is scored in three cute categories, allowing readers to compare the totals of 16 cat breeds to find out the winner"— Provided by publisher.
Identifiers: LCCN 2025012358 (print) | LCCN 2025012359 (ebook) | ISBN 9798875256509 hardcover | ISBN 9798875256455 paperback | ISBN 9798875256462 pdf | ISBN 9798875256479 epub | ISBN 9798875256486 kindle edition
Subjects: LCSH: Cat breeds—Juvenile literature | CYAC: Cat breeds | LCGFT: Picture books
Classification: LCC SF445.7 .B647 2026 (print) | LCC SF445.7 (ebook) | DDC 636.8—dc23/eng/20251124
LC record available at https://lccn.loc.gov/2025012358
LC ebook record available at https://lccn.loc.gov/2025012359

Editorial Credits
Editor: Erika L. Shores; Designer: Dina Her; Media Researcher: Rebekah Hubstenberger; Production Specialist: Tori Abraham

Image Credits
Dreamstime: © Nynke Van Holten, 12; Getty Images: iStock/GlobalP, front cover (bottom middle), back cover (top right), 11; Shutterstock: Aleks Sima, front cover (doodle bandana), chrisbrignell, 15 (cat), cynoclub, 10 (cat), Dora Zett, front cover (bottom right), Eric Isselee, 5 (cat), 13, 17, 18 (cat), Fathur Kiwon, 8 (doodle refrigerator), Kasefoto, 8 (cat), Kazantseva Olga, 19, KYRYCHENKO ANASTASIIA (doodle glasses), back cover, 5, 10, lesyau_art (stars and winner ribbon), 3, 20-21, 22-23, Look_Studio, 15 (doodle balloon), Margarita Svalova, 1 (right), 7, mholka, 6 (cat), Nadiinko (twinkle stars), front and back cover, 1, nevodka, back cover (top left), 16, Nynke van Holten, 9, Polina Tomtosova (doodle hearts, flowers, shooting star, lines), throughout, Rebellion Works, front cover (doodle bow), Sarah Fields Photography, 1 (left), 3 (left), 14, Snowice_81, 21 (cat), 22, summer studio, 6 (doodle mouse), vandycan, 3 (right), Voin_Sveta (doodle crown), front cover, 21, wabeno, front cover (bottom left), 4, Zaie (dot background), cover and throughout

Printed in the United States PO007007

CUTES FACE OFF

Cats are cute. But which cat **breed** is the Cutest Of All Time (C.O.A.T.)?

We paired 16 cuddly cats in a face-off of who's cuter. Each cat is given one to five stars in three categories. Adding up the stars gives us each cat's total cute factor. At the end, you'll use a chart to discover the C.O.A.T.!

SIAMESE

Hey! Look at meeee! Siamese cats are known for their gift of gab. They love to "chat" with their people. Some people call them "meezers." The word sounds a lot like a Siamese cat's meow.

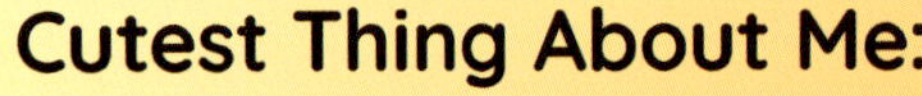

Cutest Thing About Me:
I'm always wearing a mask!

Fluffiness: ★☆☆☆☆

Aww Factor: ★★★☆☆

Cuddle-ability: ★★★☆☆

Total Cute Factor: 7

PERSIAN

Their smushy faces make them look a little grumpy. But Persians just want to be loved. Pleasing people is a Persian **trait**. It makes them easy to train. Just make sure you have plenty of treats. Come! Sit! Good kitty!

Cutest Thing About Me:
Chubby cheeks!

Fluffiness: ★★★★★

Aww Factor: ★★★☆☆

Cuddle-ability: ★★★★★

Total Cute Factor: 13

MAINE COON

That's a big kitty! Maine coons are the largest pet cats. They weigh up to 20 pounds (9 kilograms). That's as much as a small toddler. They also have fluffy fur that makes them look even bigger. Can you handle the cute?

Cutest Thing About Me:
Super fluffy neck!

Fluffiness: ★★★★★

Aww Factor: ★★★★☆

Cuddle-ability: ★★★★☆

Total Cute Factor: 13

BRITISH SHORTHAIR

These chunky cuties can come in many colors. The most common **coat** color is gray-blue. They also come in colors called **smoke**, silver, and tabby. Their eyes can be blue, green, gold, or orange. What's your favorite color combo?

Cutest Thing About Me:
Chipmunk cheeks!

Fluffiness: ★★★☆☆

Aww Factor: ★★★★☆

Cuddle-ability: ★★★★☆

Total Cute Factor: 11

ABYSSINIAN

These graceful cats are always on the go. Abyssinians love to climb, chase, and play. They will hang out on the highest spot they can reach. Where's your cat? Check on top of the fridge!

Cutest Thing About Me:
Enormous ears!

Fluffiness: ★☆☆☆☆

Aww Factor: ★★☆☆☆

Cuddle-ability: ★★★☆☆

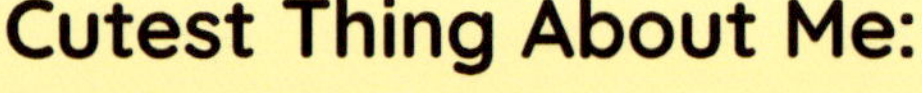

Total Cute Factor: 6

RAGDOLL

It's so fluffy! And floppy! Ragdoll cats get their name from what happens when you pick them up. They go **limp** like a ragdoll. People can carry these big kitties like a baby!

Cutest Thing About Me:
Bright blue eyes!

Fluffiness: ★★★★★
Aww Factor: ★★★★★
Cuddle-ability: ★★★★★

Total Cute Factor: 15

SPHYNX

Sphynx don't have fluffy fur. But Sphynx cats aren't totally hairless. They are covered in peach-like fuzz. Without long fur, Sphynx can get dirty. People have to give their Sphynx baths. So clean and soft!

Cutest Thing About Me:
Wrinkles, wrinkles, wrinkles!

Fluffiness: ☆☆☆☆☆
Aww Factor: ★☆☆☆☆
Cuddle-ability: ★★★☆☆

Total Cute Factor: 4

SCOTTISH FOLD

Scottish fold kittens are born with ears that stick up. After a few weeks, their ears fold over. Their folded ears give them a surprised look. Some people call Scottish folds "lop-eared" cats.

MANX

Where's that cat's tail? Don't worry. Some Manx don't have one. People call a Manx without a tail, a rumpy. A rumpy riser has a tiny tail. Short-tailed Manx are stumpys. What's a Manx with a long tail? A longy!

SELKIRK REX

A Selkirk Rex looks like it spent time at the salon. Every hair on its body is curly. Some have wavy fur. Others have tight, woolly fur. Who wouldn't want to pet a Selkirk Rex?

Cutest Thing About Me:
So much fur!

Fluffiness: ★★★★★
Aww Factor: ★★★☆☆
Cuddle-ability: ★★★☆☆

Total Cute Factor: 11

EGYPTIAN MAU

These cats date back to ancient Egypt. They are the oldest cat breed in the world. Both their fur and their skin have spots. Maus are the only cat breed with natural spots.

Cutest Thing About Me:
Polka-dot spots!

Fluffiness: ★☆☆☆☆

Aww Factor: ★★★☆☆

Cuddle-ability: ★★★☆☆

Total Cute Factor: 7

SINGAPURA

Want to cuddle the smallest kind of cat? Find a Singapura! This itty-bitty kitty weighs only 4 to 8 pounds (1.8 to 3.6 kg).

Cutest Thing About Me:
So small!

Fluffiness: ★☆☆☆☆
Aww Factor: ★★★★☆
Cuddle-ability: ★★★★☆

Total Cute Factor: 9

SNOWSHOE

Did that cat just walk through fresh snow? Snowshoes are named for their white feet. These sweet cats have dark heads, tails, and legs. Snowshoe kittens are born all white. Their fur gets darker after three weeks.

Cutest Thing About Me:
Mitten feet!

Fluffiness:	★★☆☆☆
Aww Factor:	★★★★★
Cuddle-ability:	★★★★☆

Total Cute Factor: 11

DOMESTIC SHORTHAIR

A cat that does not belong to any breed is a domestic shorthair (DSH). These friendly furballs have round heads and round eyes. Some DSHs are tabbies. A tabby has an M marking on its forehead and a striped coat.

NORWEGIAN FOREST CAT

Also called Wegies, these big cats are covered in two layers of fur. The top coat keeps out water. The undercoat is woolly and warm. Ready to cuddle? Call a Wegie!

Cutest Thing About Me:
Long, bushy fur coat!

Fluffiness: ★★★★★

Aww Factor: ★★★★☆

Cuddle-ability: ★★★★★

Total Cute Factor: 14

RUSSIAN BLUE

No other cat looks quite like a Russian Blue. Their silvery coats and bright yellow-green eyes make them stand out. These beauties can learn tricks. Some like to play fetch.

Cutest Thing About Me:
Big, A-shaped ears!

Fluffiness: ★☆☆☆☆

Aww Factor: ★★★★☆

Cuddle-ability: ★★★☆☆

Total Cute Factor: 8

CUTE FACTOR FACE OFF

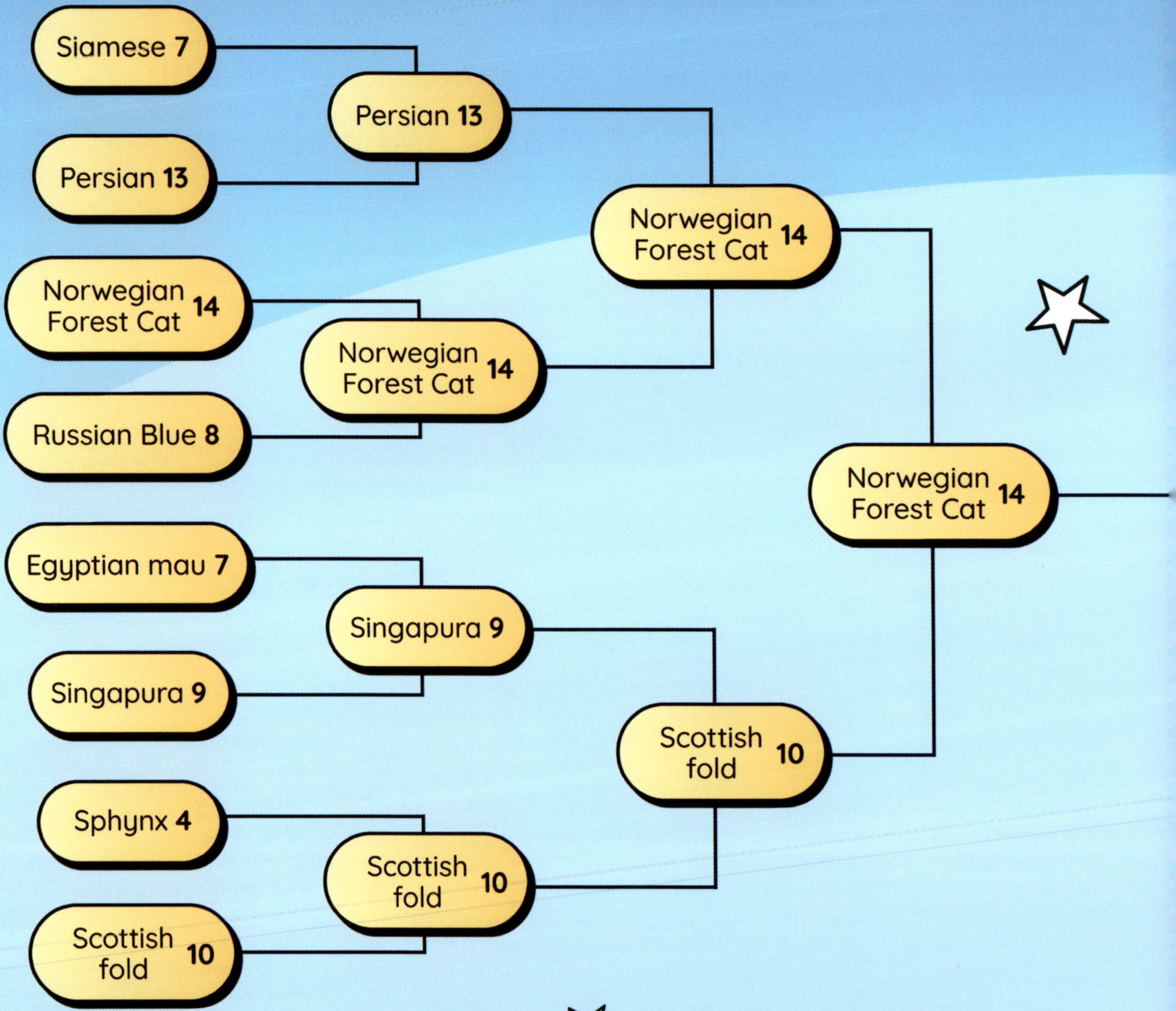

Round 1	Round 2	Semifinal	Final
Siamese 7	Persian 13	Norwegian Forest Cat 14	Norwegian Forest Cat 14
Persian 13			
Norwegian Forest Cat 14	Norwegian Forest Cat 14		
Russian Blue 8			
Egyptian mau 7	Singapura 9	Scottish fold 10	
Singapura 9			
Sphynx 4	Scottish fold 10		
Scottish fold 10			

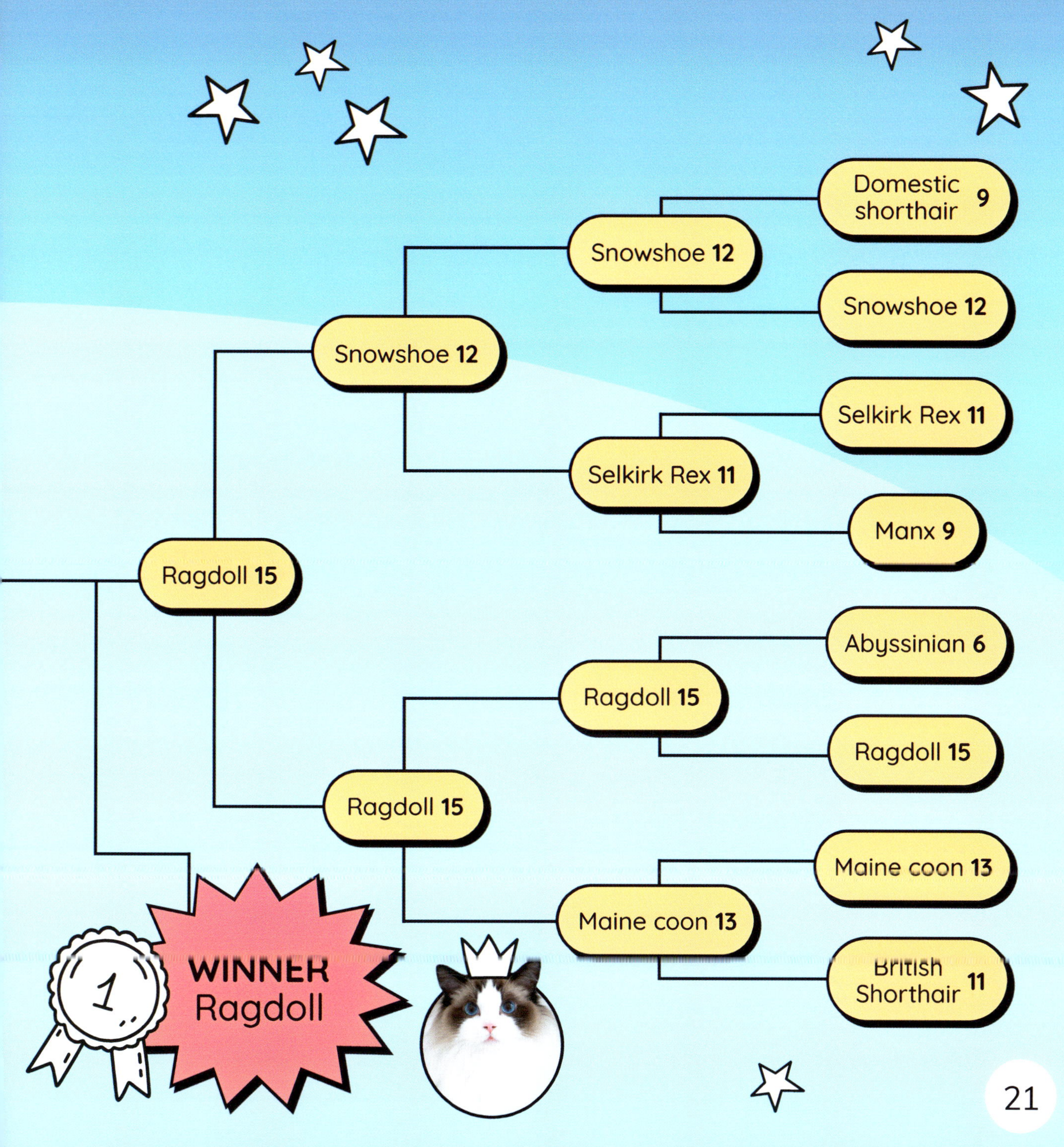
Domestic shorthair 9
Snowshoe 12
Snowshoe 12
Selkirk Rex 11
Manx 9
Abyssinian 6
Ragdoll 15
Maine coon 13
British Shorthair 11
Snowshoe 12
Selkirk Rex 11
Ragdoll 15
Maine coon 13
Snowshoe 12
Ragdoll 15
Ragdoll 15
1
WINNER
Ragdoll

THE C.O.A.T.

It's chunky. It's cuddly. It's purr-fectly precious! Its total cute factor makes it our winner. Ragdolls are the Cutest Of All Time!

Do you agree? Go back and give each cat your own score. Grab a sheet of paper and make a new chart. Maybe a different fluffy friend will be your winner.

GLOSSARY

breed (BREED)—a group of animals within a species that share the same features, such as color or markings

coat (KOHT)—an animal's hair or fur

limp (LIMP)—unmoving, without stiffness or firmness

smoke (SMOWK)—a coat pattern where only the tips of the hair is colored; the rest of the hair is white

trait (TRATE)—a feature or quality about something that makes it different from others

INDEX

ABOUT THE AUTHOR

Mari Bolte is the author and editor of hundreds of children's books. Every book is her favorite book as long as the readers learned something and enjoyed themselves!